CLASSICAL THEMES

FOR
ELECTRIC BASS

Arrangements by Mark Phillips

ISBN 978-1-4950-8911-4

7777 W. BLUEMOUND RD. P.O. BOX 13819 MILWAUKEE, WI 53213

In Australia Contact:
Hal Leonard Australia Pty. Ltd.
4 Lentara Court
Cheltenham, Victoria, 3192 Australia
Email: ausadmin@halleonard.com.au

Visit Hal Leonard Online at
www.halleonard.com

CONTENTS

Air on the G String

from ORCHESTRAL SUITE NO. 3

By Johann Sebastian Bach

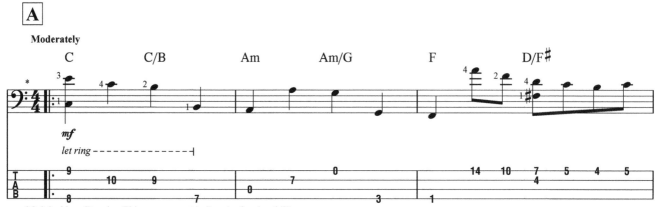

*Original key: D major. This arrangement in C major for playability.

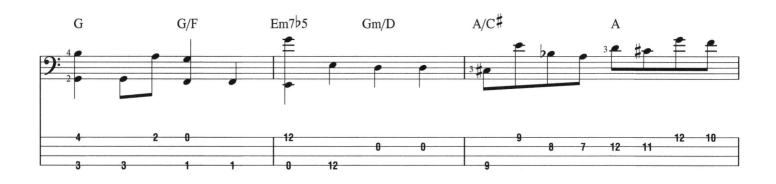

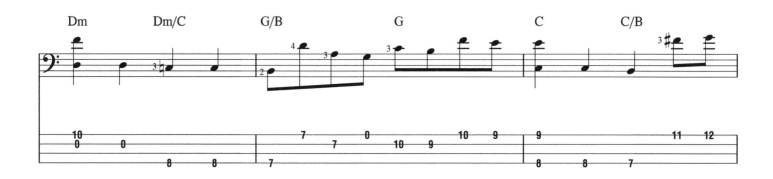

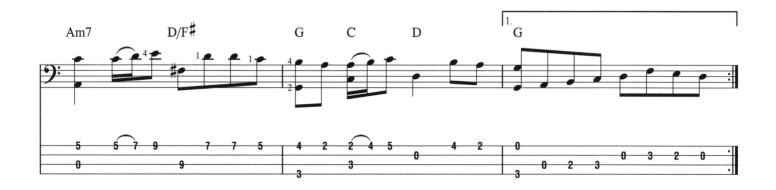

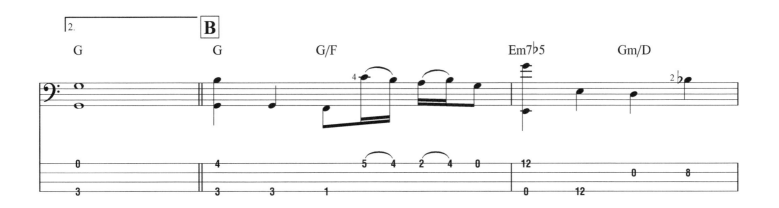

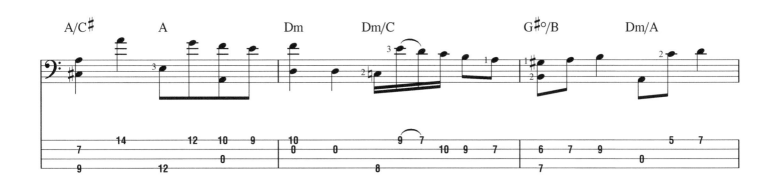

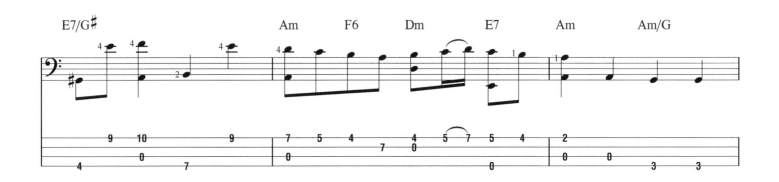

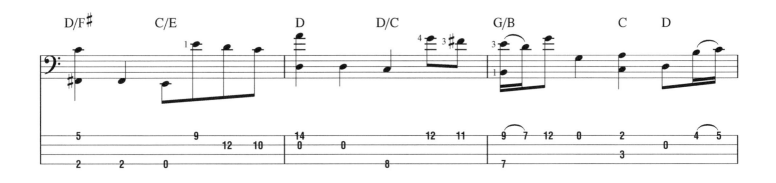

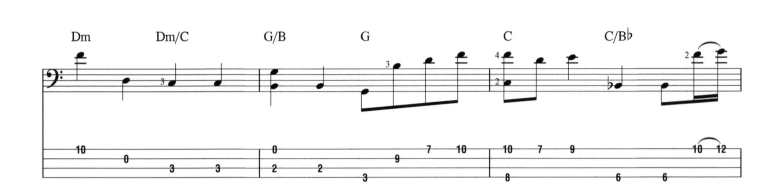

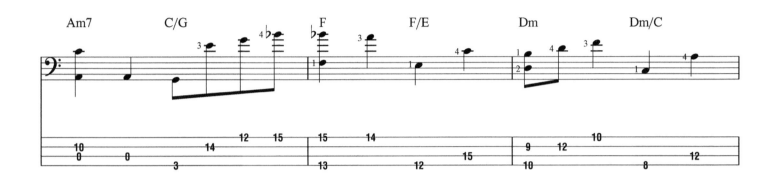

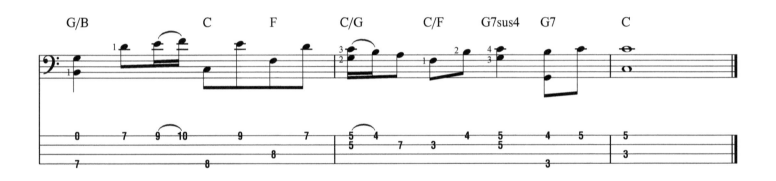

Für Elise

By Ludwig van Beethoven

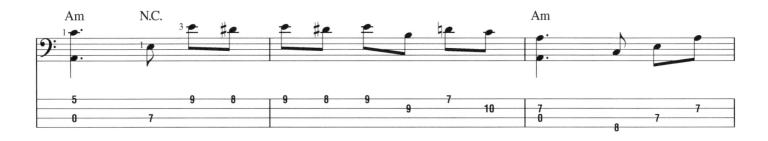

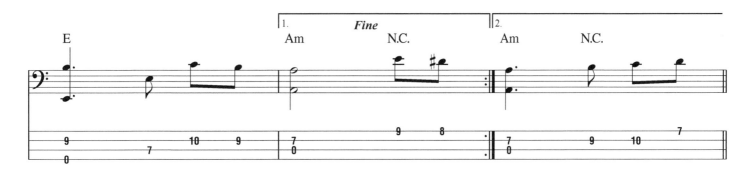

D.S. al Fine
(take 1st ending)

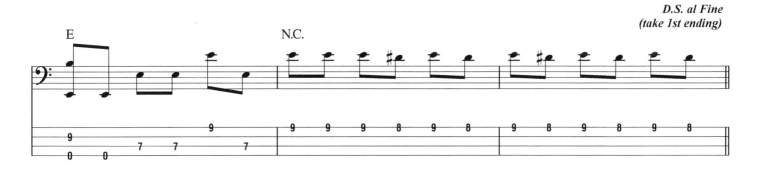

Blue Danube Waltz

By Johann Strauss, Jr.

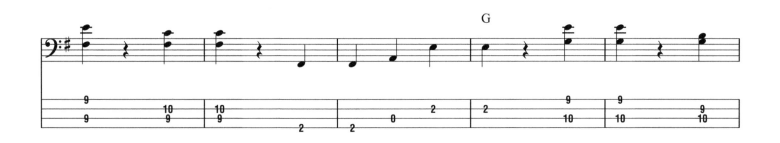

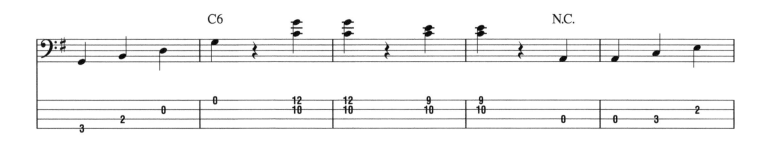

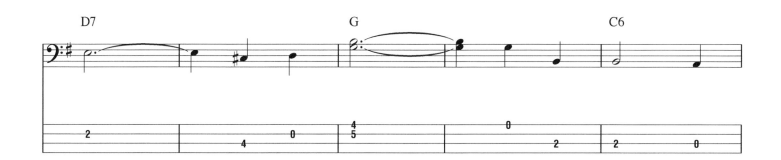

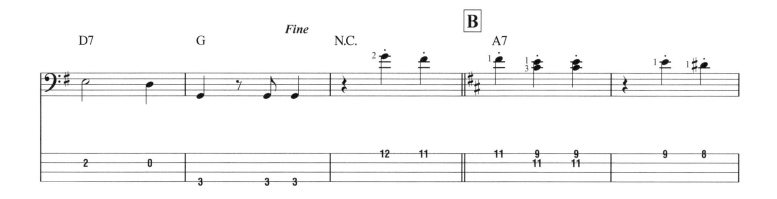

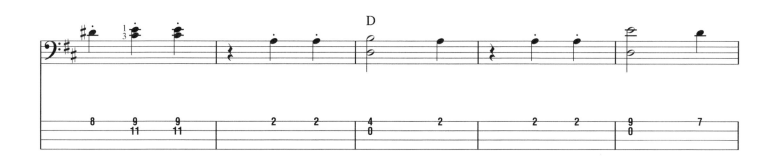

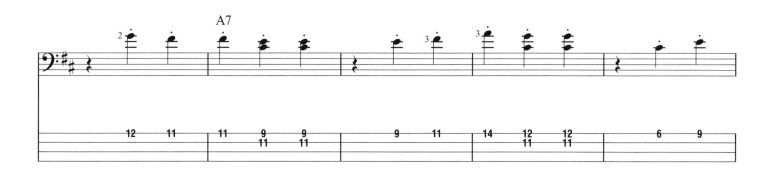

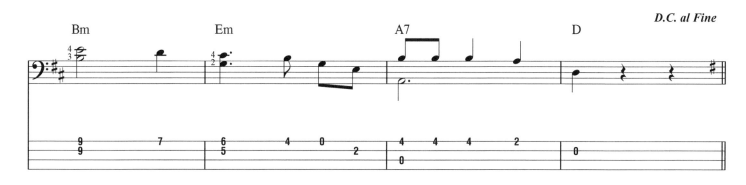

Canon in D

By Johann Pachelbel

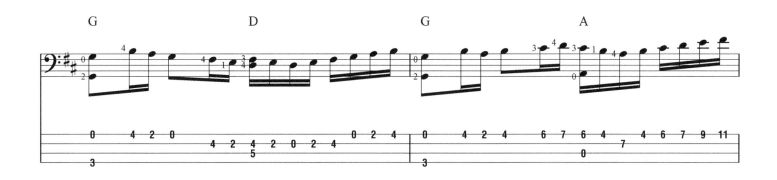

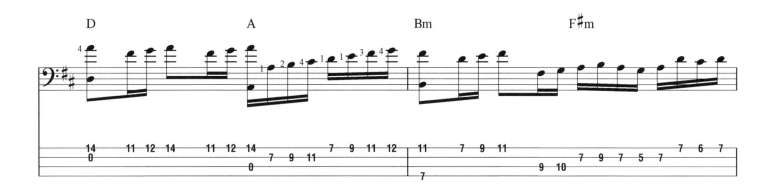

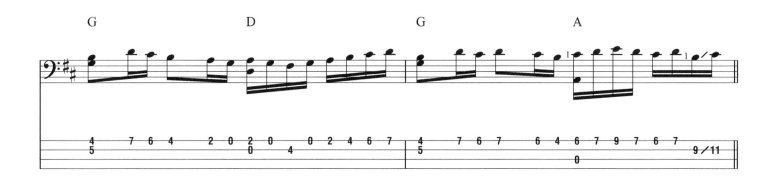

E

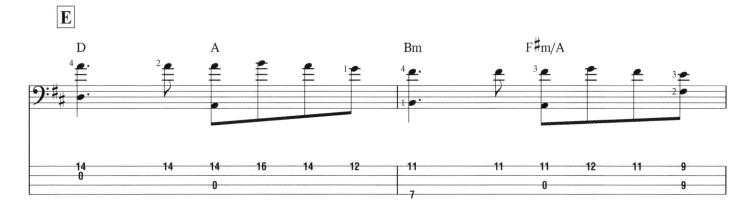

D.S. al Coda

Coda

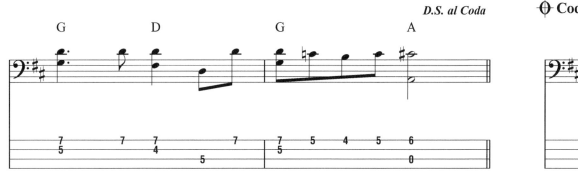

Dance of the Sugar Plum Fairy

from THE NUTCRACKER

By Pyotr Il'yich Tchaikovsky

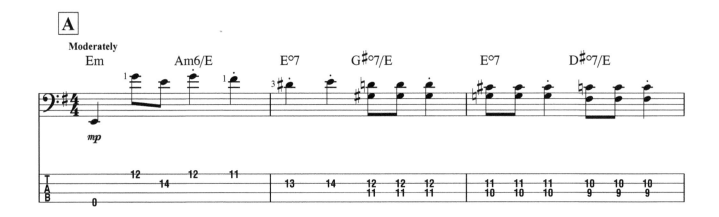

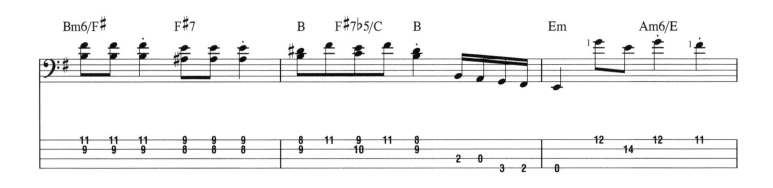

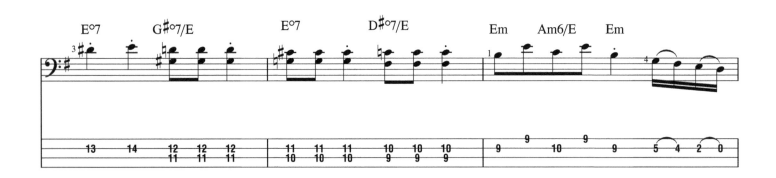

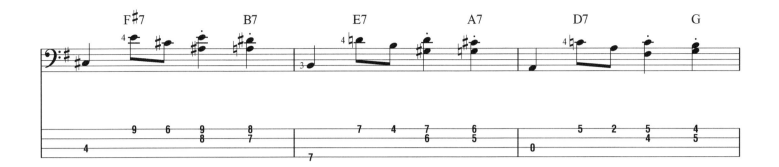

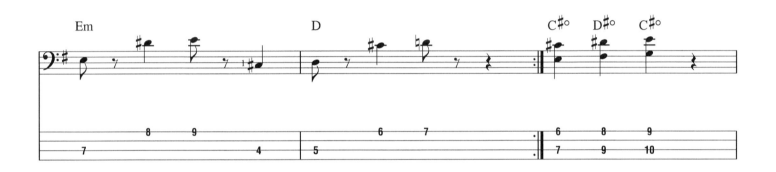

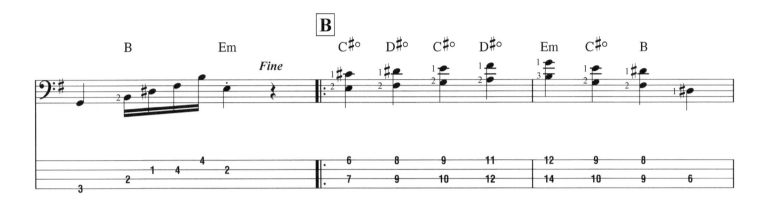

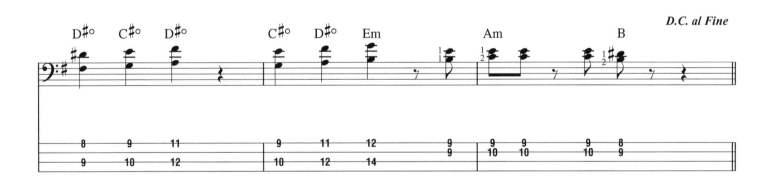

Gypsy Rondo

By Franz Joseph Haydn

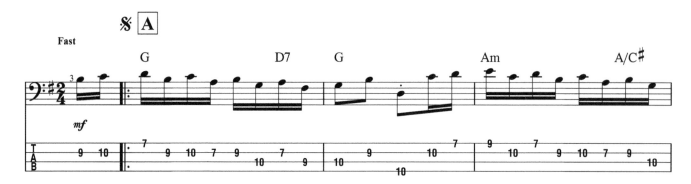

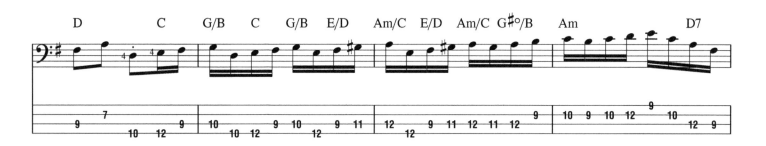

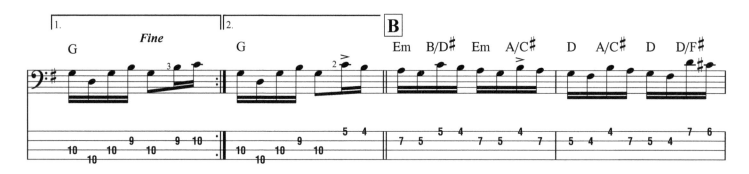

Ode to Joy

from SYMPHONY NO. 9 IN D MINOR, FOURTH MOVEMENT CHORAL THEME

By Ludwig van Beethoven

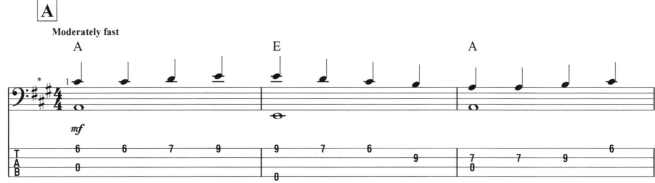

A Moderately fast

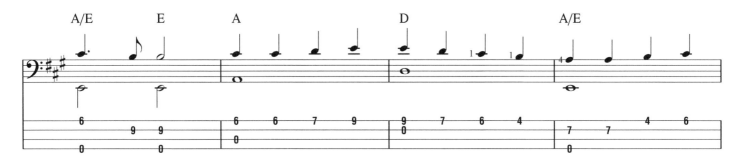

*Original key: D major. This arrangement in A major for playability.

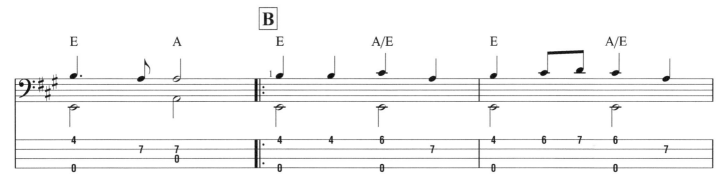

B

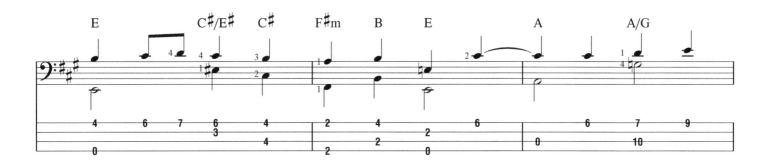

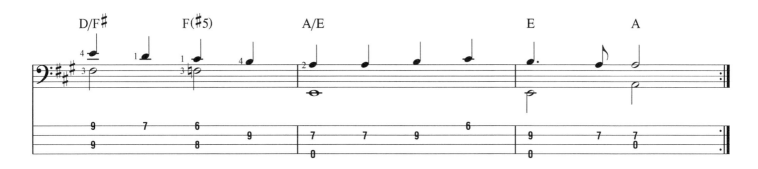

Humoresque

By Antonín Dvořák

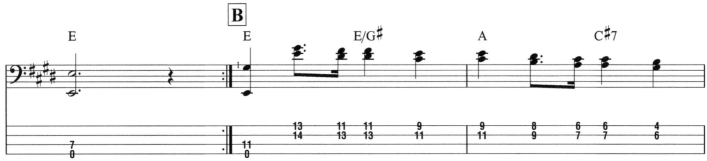

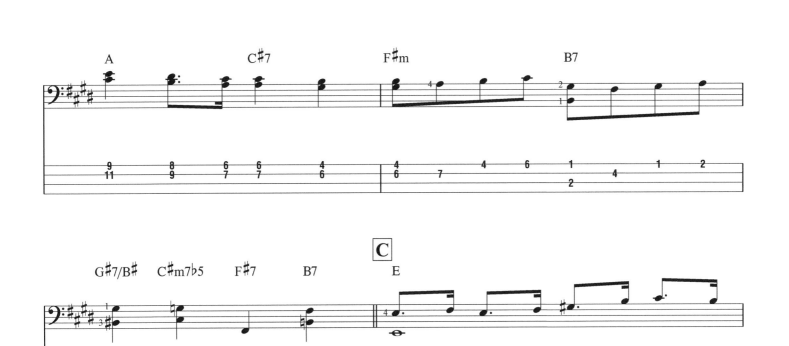

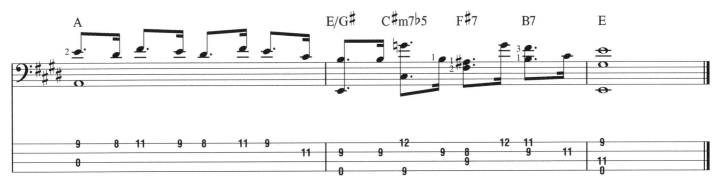

In the Hall of the Mountain King

from PEER GYNT

By Edvard Grieg

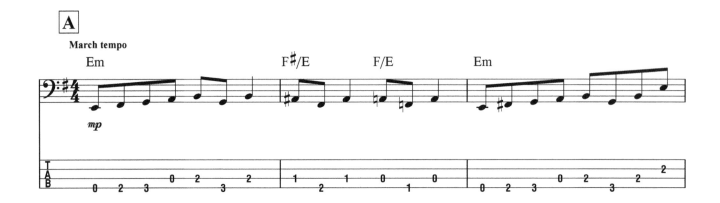

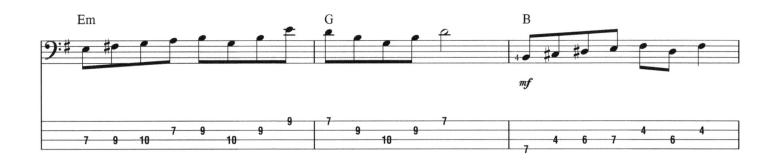

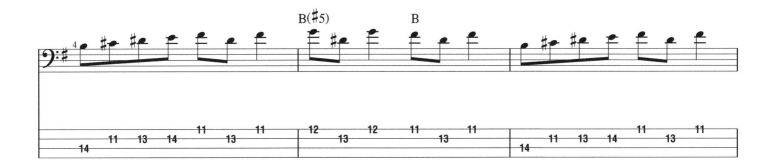

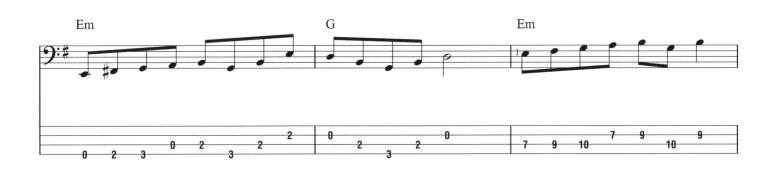

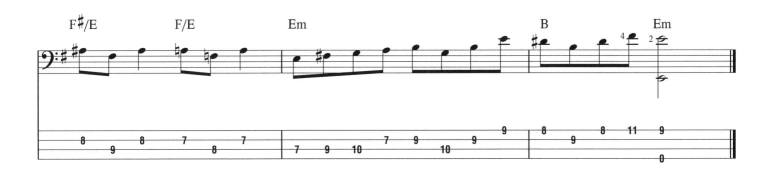

Jesu, Joy of Man's Desiring

By Johann Sebastian Bach

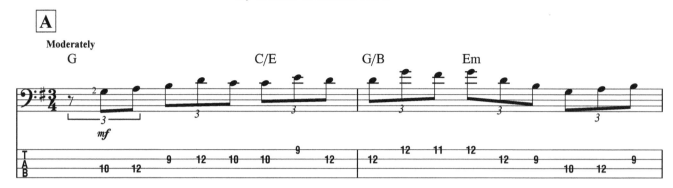

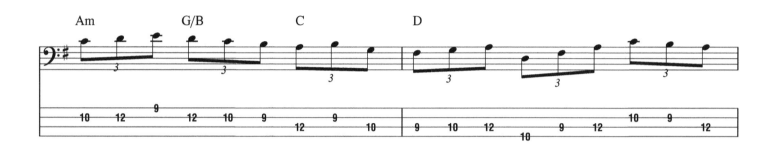

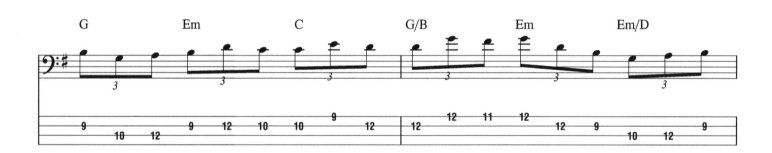

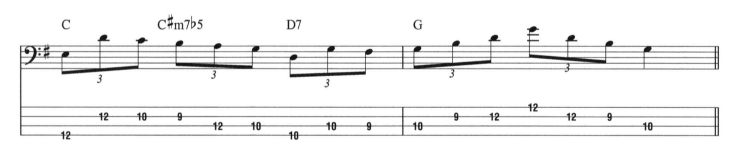

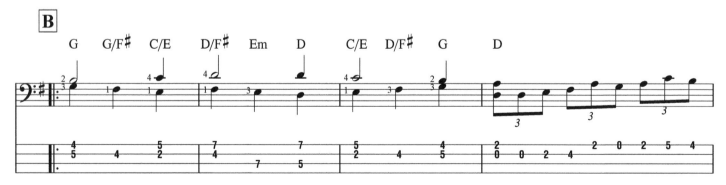

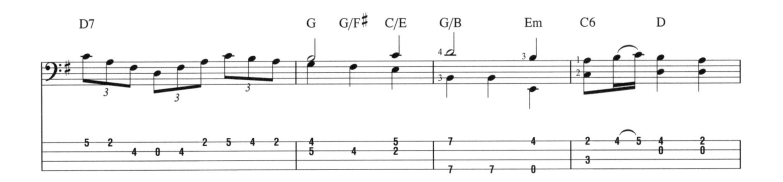

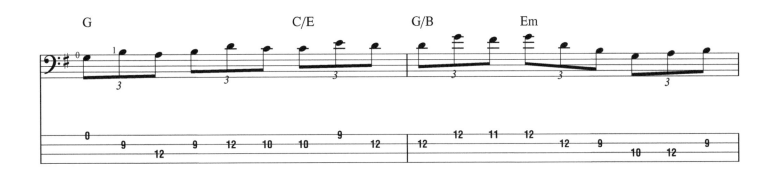

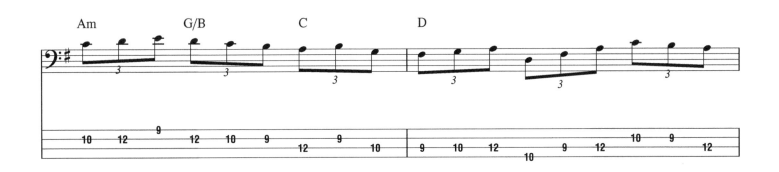

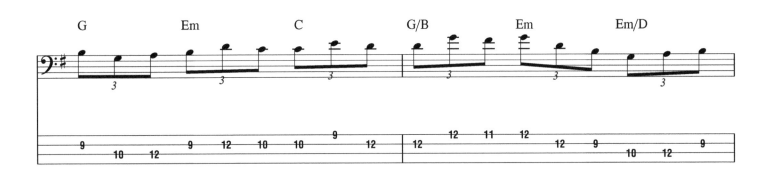

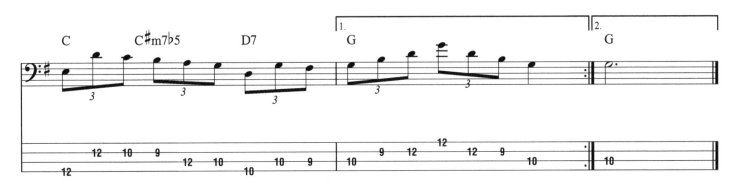

Minuet
from THE STRING QUINTET IN E MAJOR, OP. 11, NO. 5
By Luigi Boccherini

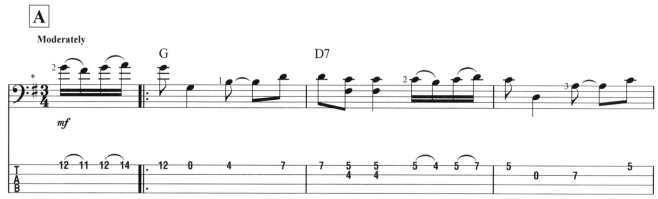

*Original key: A major. This arrangement in G major for playability.

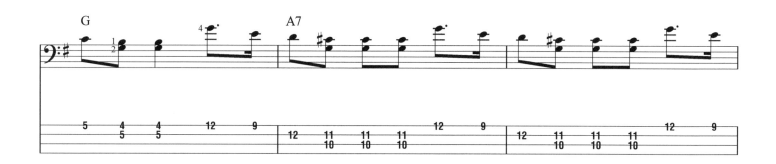

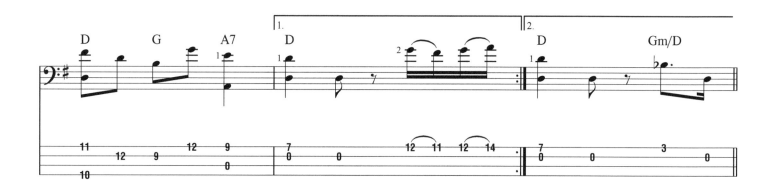

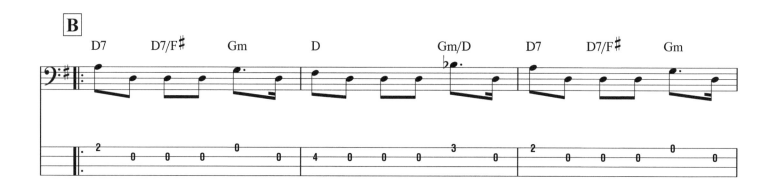

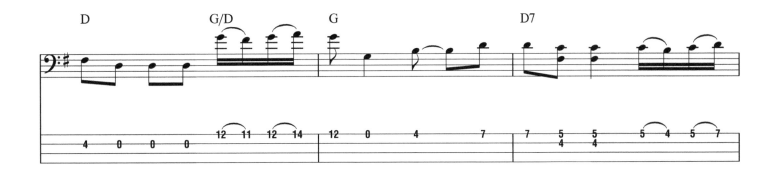

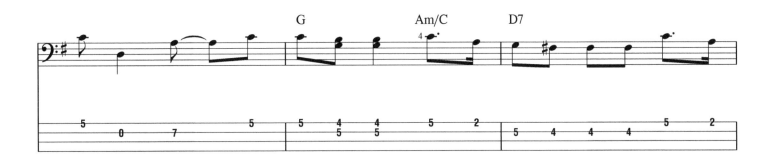

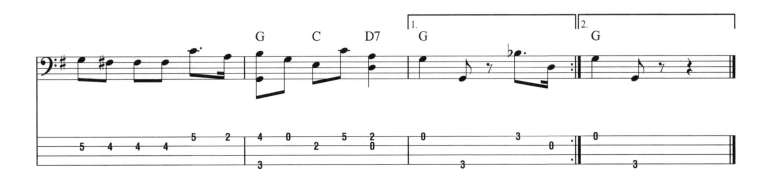

Minuet in F Major, K. 2

By Wolfgang Amadeus Mozart

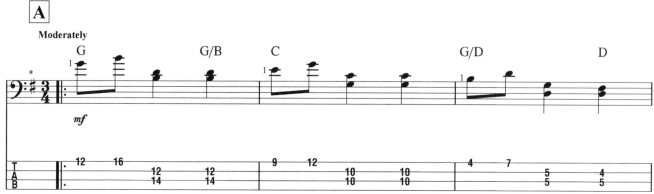

*Original key: F major. This arrangement in G major for playability.

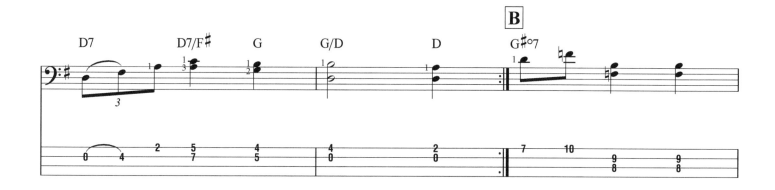

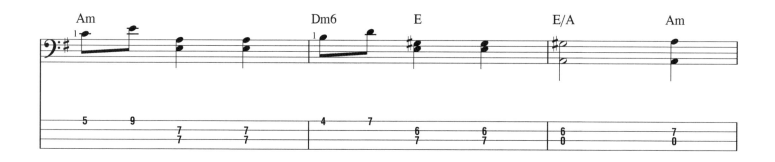

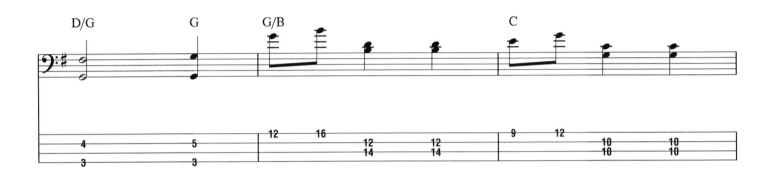

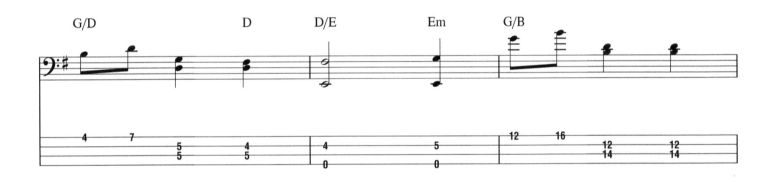

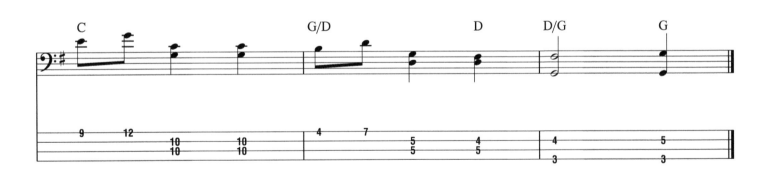

Pavane

By Gabriel Fauré

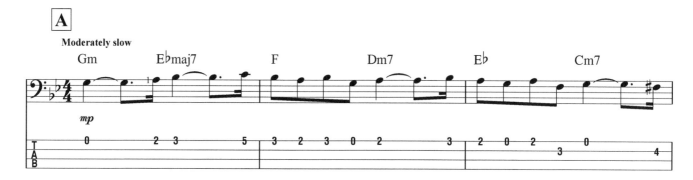

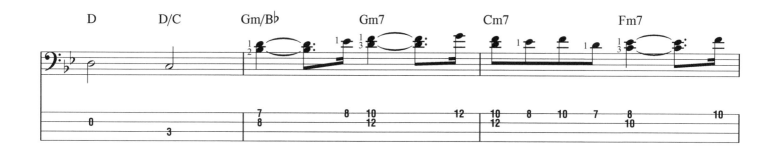

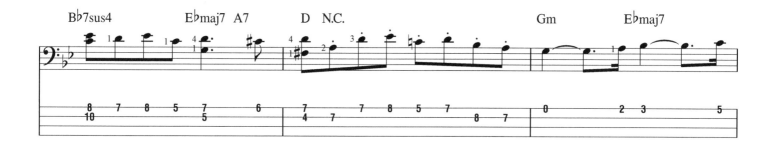

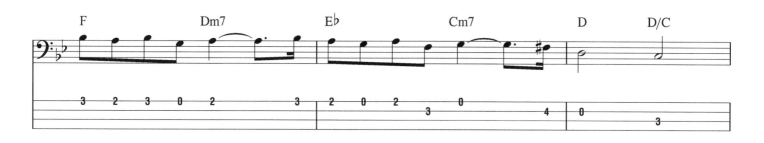

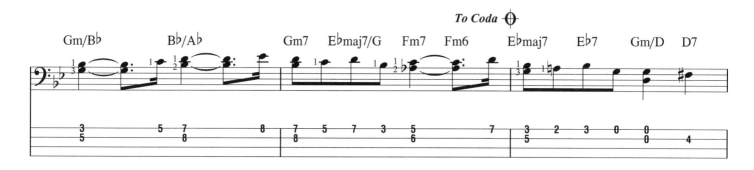

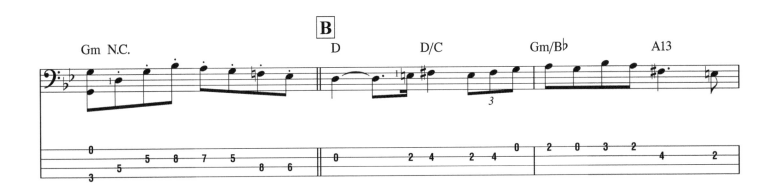

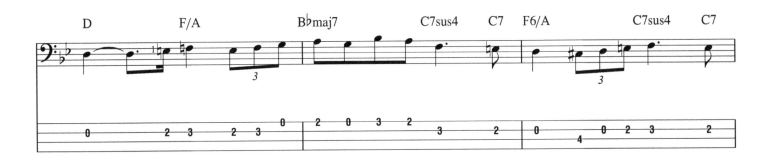

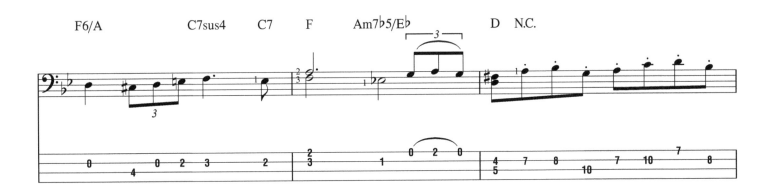

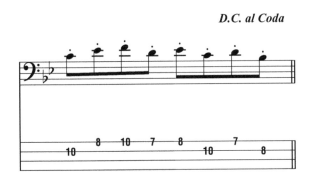

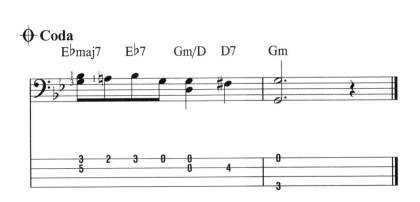

Rondeau

By Jean-Joseph Mouret

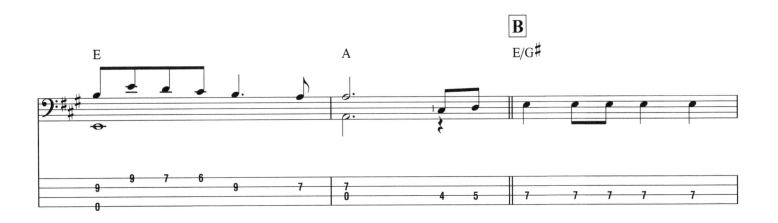

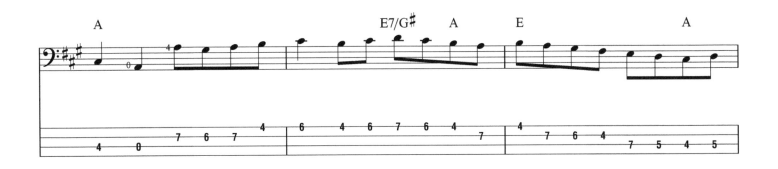

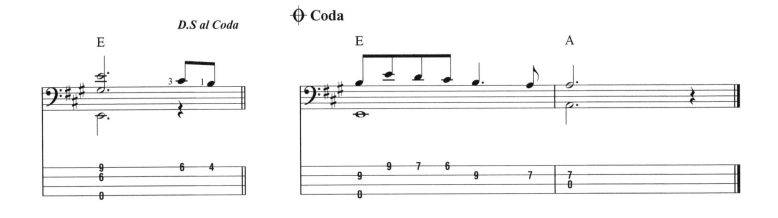

Sonatina in C Major
Op. 36, No. 1
By Muzio Clementi

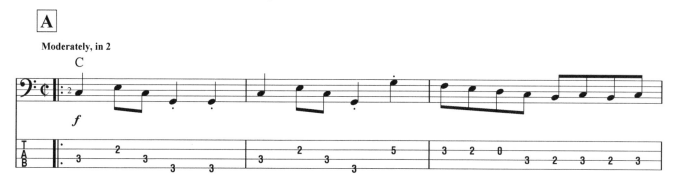

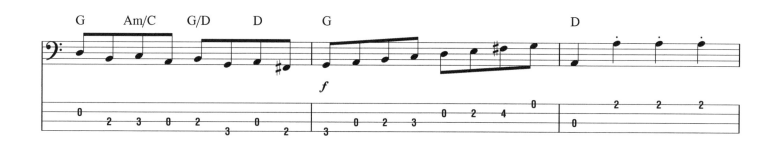

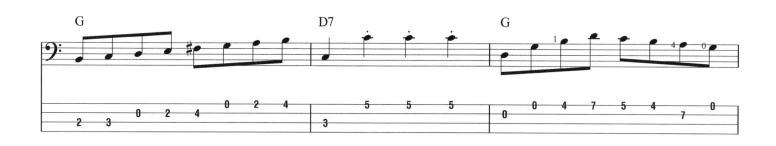

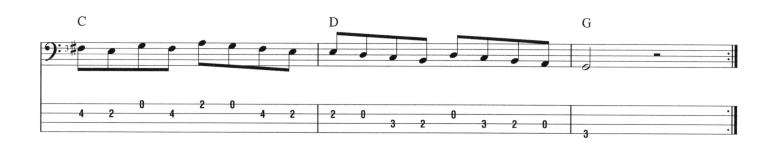

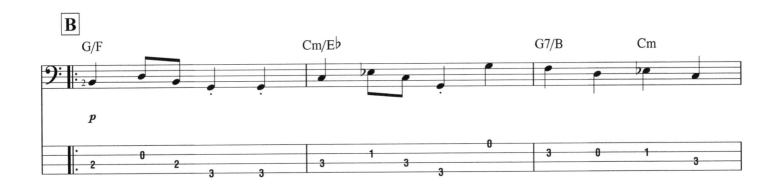

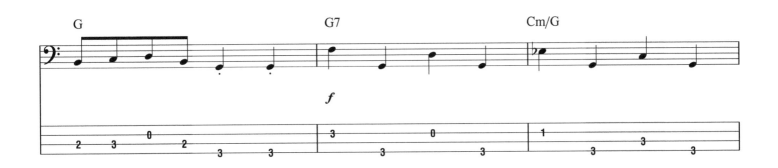

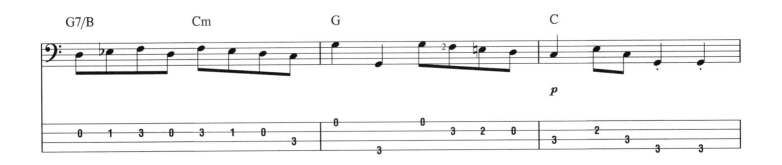

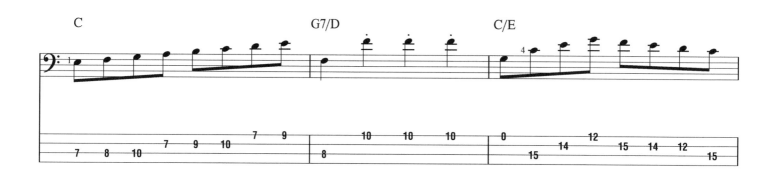

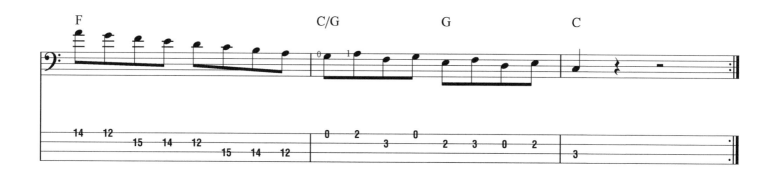

Spring

from THE FOUR SEASONS

(First Movement Theme)

By Antonio Vivaldi

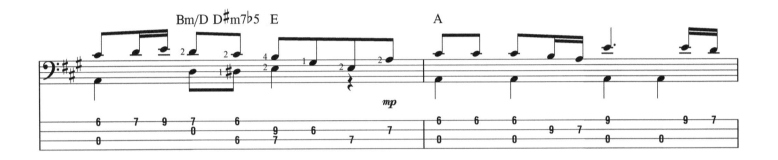

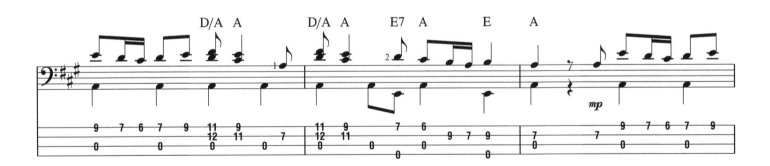

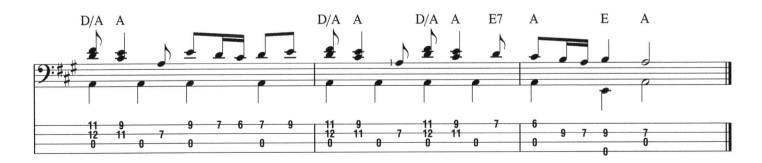

Spring Song

Op. 62, No. 6

from SONGS WITHOUT WORDS

By Felix Mendelssohn

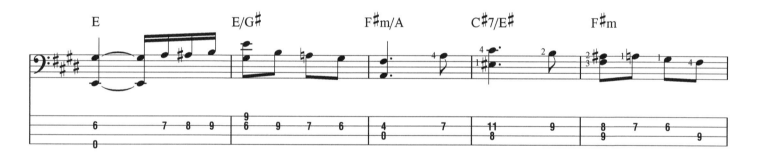

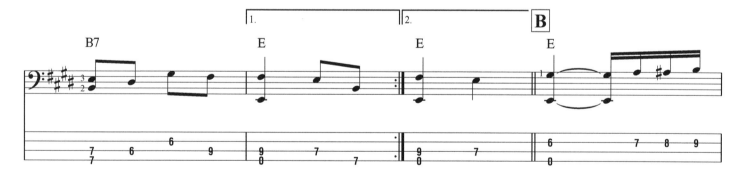

Toreador Song

from CARMEN

By Georges Bizet

Toccata and Fugue in D Minor

By Johann Sebastian Bach

Drop D tuning:
(low to high) D-A-D-G

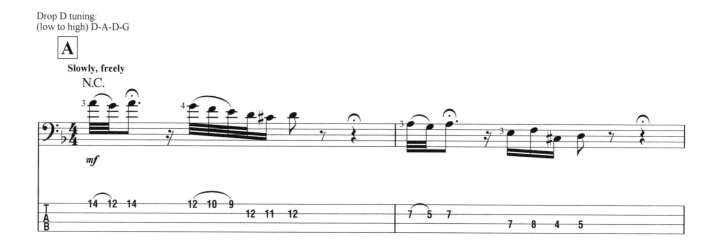

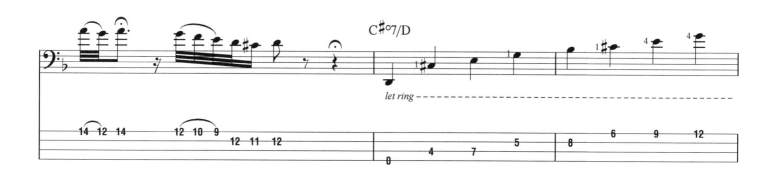

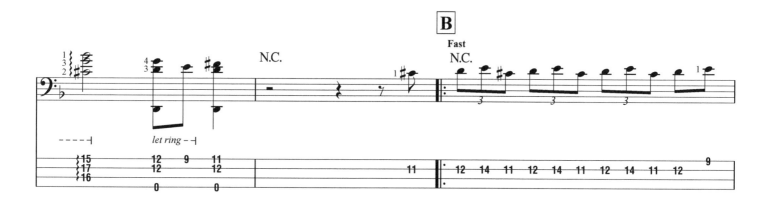

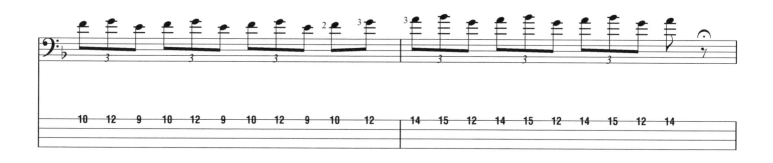

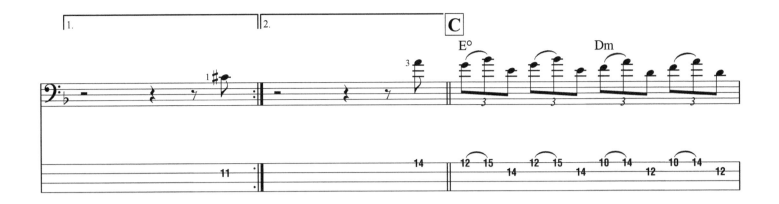

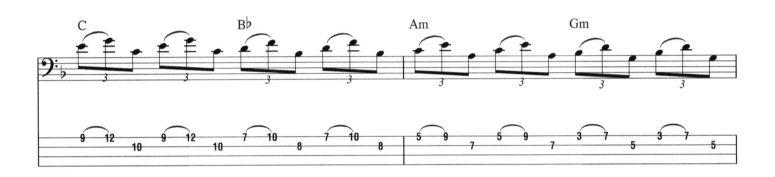

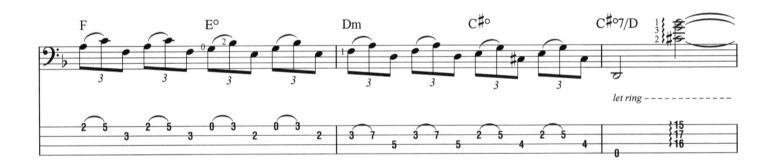

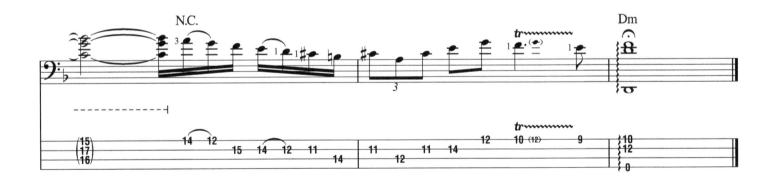

Turkish Rondo
from SONATA IN A MAJOR, K. 331, THIRD MOVEMENT EXCERPT
By Wolfgang Amadeus Mozart

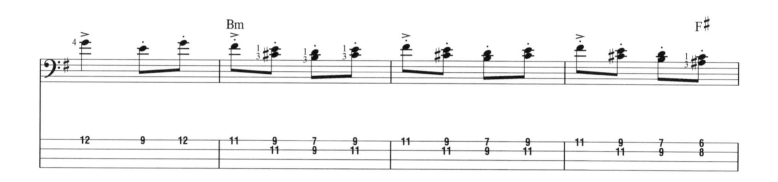

*Original key: A minor. This arrangement in E minor for playability.

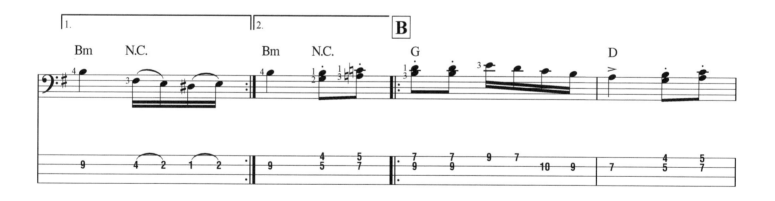

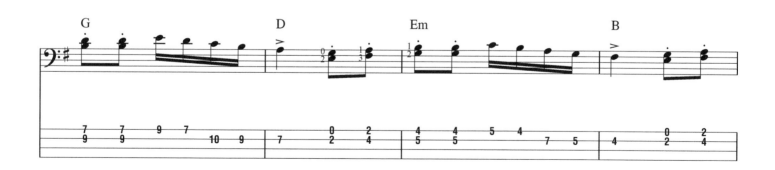

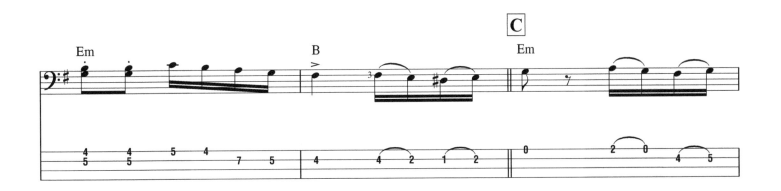

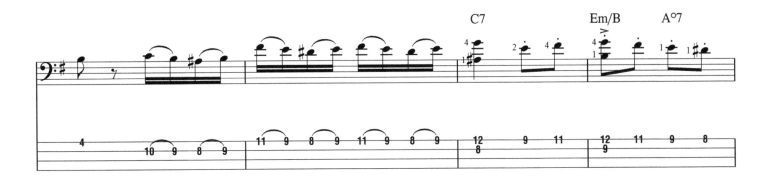

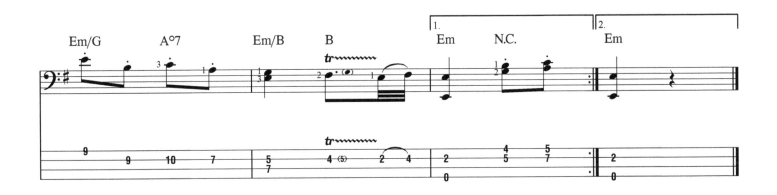

BASS NOTATION LEGEND

Bass music can be notated two different ways: on a *musical staff*, and in *tablature*.

THE MUSICAL STAFF shows pitches and rhythms and is divided by bar lines into measures. Pitches are named after the first seven letters of the alphabet.

TABLATURE graphically represents the bass fingerboard. Each horizontal line represents a string, and each number represents a fret.

3rd string, open   2nd string, 2nd fret   1st & 2nd strings open, played together

HAMMER-ON: Strike the first (lower) note with one finger, then sound the higher note (on the same string) with another finger by fretting it without picking.

PULL-OFF: Place both fingers on the notes to be sounded. Strike the first note and without picking, pull the finger off to sound the second (lower) note.

LEGATO SLIDE: Strike the first note and then slide the same fret-hand finger up or down to the second note. The second note is not struck.

SHIFT SLIDE: Same as legato slide, except the second note is struck.

TRILL: Very rapidly alternate between the notes indicated by continuously hammering on and pulling off.

TREMOLO PICKING: The note is picked as rapidly and continuously as possible.

VIBRATO: The string is vibrated by rapidly bending and releasing the note with the fretting hand.

SHAKE: Using one finger, rapidly alternate between two notes on one string by sliding either a half-step above or below.

NATURAL HARMONIC: Strike the note while the fret hand lightly touches the string directly over the fret indicated.

Harm.

MUFFLED STRINGS: A percussive sound is produced by laying the fret hand across the string(s) without depressing them and striking them with the pick hand.

BEND: Strike the note and bend up the interval shown.

1/2

BEND AND RELEASE: Strike the note and bend up as indicated, then release back to the original note. Only the first note is struck.

1/2

RIGHT-HAND TAP: Hammer ("tap") the fret indicated with the "pick-hand" index or middle finger and pull off to the note fretted by the fret hand.

+

LEFT-HAND TAP: Hammer ("tap") the fret indicated with the "fret-hand" index or middle finger.

⊕

SLAP: Strike ("slap") string with right-hand thumb.

T

POP: Snap ("pop") string with right-hand index or middle finger.

P

Additional Musical Definitions

(accent) • Accentuate note (play it louder).

^
(accent) • Accentuate note with great intensity.

•
(staccato) • Play the note short.

⊓
• Downstroke

V
• Upstroke

D.S. al Coda
• Go back to the sign (𝄋), then play until the measure marked "**To Coda**," then skip to the section labelled "**Coda**."

D.C. al Fine
• Go back to the beginning of the song and play until the measure marked "*Fine*" (end).

Bass Fig.
• Label used to recall a recurring pattern.

Fill
• Label used to identify a brief melodic figure which is to be inserted into the arrangement.

tacet
• Instrument is silent (drops out).

• Repeat measures between signs.

1. 2.
• When a repeated section has different endings, play the first ending only the first time and the second ending only the second time.

NOTE: Tablature numbers in parentheses mean:
1. The note is being sustained over a system (note in standard notation is tied), or
2. The note is sustained, but a new articulation (such as a hammer-on, pull-off, slide or vibrato) begins.